ESSENTIAL SONGS FOR
alto sax

Available for
FLUTE, CLARINET, ALTO SAX, TENOR SAX, TRUMPET,
HORN, TROMBONE, VIOLIN, VIOLA, CELLO

ISBN 978-1-4234-5533-2

Visit Hal Leonard Online at
www.halleonard.com

Contact Us:
Hal Leonard
7777 West Bluemound Road
Milwaukee, WI 53213
Email: info@halleonard.com

In Europe contact:
Hal Leonard Europe Limited
42 Wigmore Street
Marylebone, London, W1U 2RN
Email: info@halleonardeurope.com

In Australia contact:
Hal Leonard Australia Pty. Ltd.
4 Lentara Court
Cheltenham, Victoria, 3192 Australia
Email: info@halleonard.com.au

CONTENTS

ALL SHOOK UP

ALTO SAX

Words and Music by OTIS BLACKWELL
and ELVIS PRESLEY

ALL THE WAY
from THE JOKER IS WILD

ALTO SAX

Words by SAMMY CAHN
Music by JAMES VEN HEUSEN

AND I LOVE HER

ALTO SAX

Words and Music by JOHN LENNON
and PAUL McCARTNEY

ANYONE CAN WHISTLE

from ANYONE CAN WHISTLE

ALTO SAX

Words and Music by
STEPHEN SONDHEIM

Slowly and tenderly

AUTUMN LEAVES

ALTO SAX

English lyrics by JOHNNY MERCER
French lyrics by JACQUES PREVERT
Music by JOSEPH KOSMA

Slowly, with expression

BABY, I LOVE YOUR WAY

ALTO SAX

Words and Music by
PETER FRAMPTON

BACK AT ONE

ALTO SAX

Words and Music by
BRIAN McKNIGHT

BEAUTIFUL

ALTO SAX

Words and Music by
LINDA PERRY

BECAUSE OF YOU

ALTO SAX

Words and Music by KELLY CLARKSON,
DAVID HODGES and BEN MOODY

BENNIE AND THE JETS

ALTO SAX

Words and Music by ELTON JOHN
and BERNIE TAUPIN

BLESS THE BROKEN ROAD

ALTO SAX

Words and Music by MARCUS HUMMON,
BOBBY BOYD and JEFF HANNA

15

BORN FREE

from the Columbia Pictures' Release BORN FREE

ALTO SAX

Words by DON BLACK
Music by JOHN BARRY

BRING HIM HOME

from LES MISÉRABLES

ALTO SAX

Music by CLAUDE-MICHEL SCHÖNBERG
Lyrics by HERBERT KRETZMER and ALAIN BOUBLIL

BREATHE

ALTO SAX

Words and Music by HOLLY LAMAR
and STEPHANIE BENTLEY

BYE BYE LOVE

ALTO SAX

Words and Music by FELICE BRYANT
and BOUDLEAUX BRYANT

CALIFORNIA GIRLS

ALTO SAX

Words and Music by BRIAN WILSON
and MIKE LOVE

CAN YOU FEEL THE LOVE TONIGHT

from Walt Disney Pictures' THE LION KING

ALTO SAX

Music by ELTON JOHN
Lyrics by TIM RICE

THE CHICKEN DANCE

ALTO SAX

By TERRY RENDALL
and WERNER THOMAS

CLIMB EV'RY MOUNTAIN

from THE SOUND OF MUSIC

ALTO SAX

Lyrics by OSCAR HAMMERSTEIN II
Music by RICHARD RODGERS

CRAZY LITTLE THING CALLED LOVE

ALTO SAX

Words and Music by
FREDDIE MERCURY

COMPLICATED

Alto Sax

Words and Music by AVRIL LAVIGNE,
LAUREN CHRISTY, SCOTT SPOCK
and GRAHAM EDWARDS

D.S. al Coda

CODA

CROCODILE ROCK

ALTO SAX

Words and Music by ELTON JOHN
and BERNIE TAUPIN

DANCING QUEEN

ALTO SAX

Words and Music by BENNY ANDERSSON,
BJORN ULVAEUS and STIG ANDERSON

Strong Rock

DON'T KNOW WHY

ALTO SAX

Words and Music by
JESSE HARRIS

DREAM LOVER

ALTO SAX

Words and Music by
BOBBY DARIN

Moderately

DROPS OF JUPITER
(Tell Me)

ALTO SAX

Words and Music by PAT MONAHAN,
JIMMY STAFFORD, ROB HOTCHKISS,
CHARLIE COLIN and SCOTT UNDERWOOD

Moderately

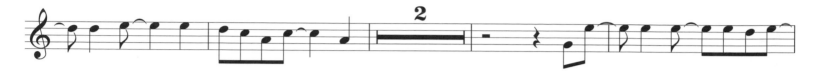

D.S. al Coda

CODA

DUST IN THE WIND

ALTO SAX

Words and Music by
KERRY LIVGREN

EASTER PARADE

from AS THOUSANDS CHEER

ALTO SAX

Words and Music by
IRVING BERLIN

Moderately

ENDLESS LOVE

ALTO SAX

Words and Music by
LIONEL RICHIE

FEVER

ALTO SAX

Words and Music by JOHN DAVENPORT
and EDDIE COOLEY

FIRE AND RAIN

ALTO SAX

Words and Music by
JAMES TAYLOR

THE FIRST CUT IS THE DEEPEST

ALTO SAX

Words and Music by
CAT STEVENS

THE FOOL ON THE HILL

ALTO SAX

Words and Music by JOHN LENNON
and PAUL McCARTNEY

FOOTLOOSE
Theme from the Paramount Motion Picture FOOTLOOSE

ALTO SAX

Words by DEAN PITCHFORD
and KENNY LOGGINS
Music by KENNY LOGGINS

FROM A DISTANCE

ALTO SAX

Words and Music by
JULIE GOLD

GO AWAY, LITTLE GIRL

ALTO SAX

Words and Music by GERRY GOFFIN
and CAROLE KING

GOOD VIBRATIONS

ALTO SAX

Words and Music by BRIAN WILSON
and MIKE LOVE

GOT MY MIND SET ON YOU

ALTO SAX

Words and Music by
RUDY CLARK

A GROOVY KIND OF LOVE

ALTO SAX

Words and Music by TONI WINE
and CAROLE BAYER SAGER

HAPPY TOGETHER

ALTO SAX

Words and Music by GARRY BONNER
and ALAN GORDON

HAPPY TRAILS

from the Television Series THE ROY ROGERS SHOW

ALTO SAX

Words and Music by
DALE EVANS

HEAVEN

ALTO SAX

Words and Music by BRYAN ADAMS
and JIM VALLANCE

HEAVEN

ALTO SAX

Words and Music by HENRY GARZA,
JOEY GARZA and RINGO GARZA

HELLO

ALTO SAX

Words and Music by
LIONEL RICHIE

Slow Ballad

HIGH HOPES

ALTO SAX

Words by SAMMY CAHN
Music by JAMES VAN HEUSEN

Moderately, with a beat

HOW CAN YOU MEND A BROKEN HEART

ALTO SAX

Words and Music by BARRY GIBB
and ROBIN GIBB

HOW SWEET IT IS (TO BE LOVED BY YOU)

ALTO SAX

Words and Music by EDWARD HOLLAND,
LAMONT DOZIER and BRIAN HOLLAND

I GOT YOU
(I Feel Good)

ALTO SAX

Words and Music by
JAMES BROWN

Steady Funk Rock

(Spoken:) Hey!

I HOPE YOU DANCE

ALTO SAX

Words and Music by TIA SILLERS
and MARK D. SANDERS

I JUST CALLED TO SAY I LOVE YOU

ALTO SAX

Words and Music by
STEVIE WONDER

I LEFT MY HEART IN SAN FRANCISCO

ALTO SAX

Words by DOUGLASS CROSS
Music by GEORGE CORY

I SHOT THE SHERIFF

ALTO SAX

Words and Music by
BOB MARLEY

Moderately slow, with a beat

I WANT TO HOLD YOUR HAND

ALTO SAX

Words and Music by JOHN LENNON
PAUL McCARTNEY

Moderately, with a beat

I'LL BE THERE

ALTO SAX

Words and Music by BERRY GORDY,
HAL DAVIS, WILLIE HUTCH
and BOB WEST

I'LL BE

ALTO SAX

Words and Music by
EDWIN McCAIN

I'M WITH YOU

ALTO SAX

Words and Music by AVRIL LAVIGNE, LAUREN CHRISTY,
SCOTT SPOCK and GRAHAM EDWARDS

IF

ALTO SAX

Words and Music by
DAVID GATES

Moderately, with feeling

IF I HAD A HAMMER
(The Hammer Song)

ALTO SAX

Words and Music by LEE HAYS
and PETE SEEGER

THE IMPRESSION THAT I GET

ALTO SAX

Words and Music by DICKY BARRETT
and JOE GITTLEMAN

IN THE MOOD

ALTO SAX

By JOE GARLAND

IT'S A SMALL WORLD

from "it's a small world" at Disneyland Park and Magic Kingdom Park

ALTO SAX

Words and Music by RICHARD M. SHERMAN
and ROBERT B. SHERMAN

IT'S TOO LATE

ALTO SAX

Words and Music by CAROLE KING
and TONI STERN

ITSY BITSY TEENIE WEENIE
YELLOW POLKADOT BIKINI

ALTO SAX

Words and Music by PAUL VANCE
and LEE POCKRISS

THEME FROM "JURASSIC PARK"

from the Universal Motion Picture JURASSIC PARK

ALTO SAX

Composed by
JOHN WILLIAMS

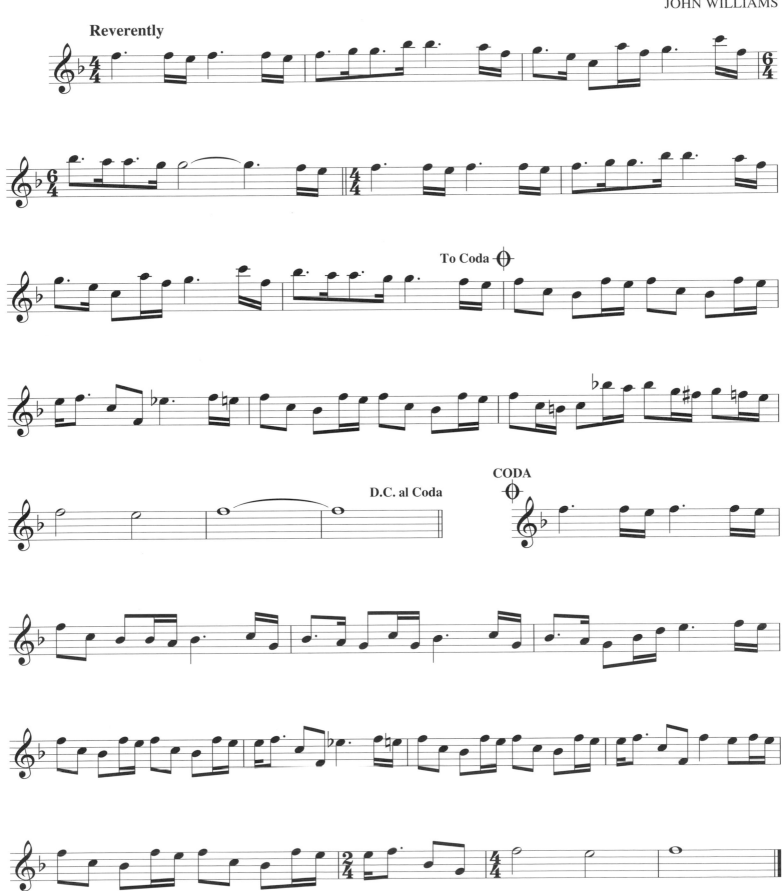

KING OF THE ROAD

ALTO SAX

Words and Music by
ROGER MILLER

LA BAMBA

ALTO SAX

By RITCHIE VALENS

LET IT BE

ALTO SAX

Words and Music by JOHN LENNON
PAUL McCARTNEY

LISTEN TO WHAT THE MAN SAID

ALTO SAX

Words and Music by
PAUL and LINDA McCARTNEY

THE LOCO-MOTION

ALTO SAX

Words and Music by GERRY GOFFIN
and CAROLE KING

LOUIE, LOUIE

ALTO SAX

Words and Music by
RICHARD BERRY

LOVE ME TENDER

ALTO SAX

Words and Music by ELVIS PRESLEY
and VERA MATSON

LUCY IN THE SKY WITH DIAMONDS

ALTO SAX

Words and Music by JOHN LENNON
and PAUL McCARTNEY

MAMBO NO. 5
(A Little Bit Of...)

ALTO SAX

Original Music by DAMASO PEREZ PRADO
Words by LOU BEGA and ZIPPY

ME AND BOBBY McGEE

ALTO SAX

Words and Music by KRIS KRISTOFFERSON
and FRED FOSTER

A MOMENT LIKE THIS

ALTO SAX

Words and Music by JOHN REID
and JORGEN KJELL ELOFSSON

Moderately slow

MY FAVORITE THINGS

from THE SOUND OF MUSIC

ALTO SAX

Lyrics by OSCAR HAMMERSTEIN II
Music by RICHARD RODGERS

THE ODD COUPLE

Theme from the Paramount Picture THE ODD COUPLE
Theme from the Paramount Television Series THE ODD COUPLE

ALTO SAX

By NEAL HEFTI

ON TOP OF SPAGHETTI

ALTO SAX

Words and Music by
TOM GLAZER

100 YEARS

ALTO SAX

Words and Music by
JOHN ONDRASIK

Moderately fast

ONE NOTE SAMBA
(Samba de uma nota so)

ALTO SAX

Original Lyrics by NEWTON MENDONCA
English Lyrics by ANTONIO CARLOS JOBIM
Music by ANTONIO CARLOS JOBIM

PETER COTTONTAIL

ALTO SAX

Words and Music by STEVE NELSON
and JACK ROLLINS

PUPPY LOVE

ALTO SAX

Words and Music by
PAUL ANKA

Moderately slow

QUE SERA, SERA
(Whatever Will Be, Will Be)
from THE MAN WHO KNEW TOO MUCH

Alto Sax

Words and Music by JAY LIVINGSTON
and RAY EVANS

R.O.C.K. IN THE U.S.A
(A Salute to 60's Rock)

ALTO SAX

Words and Music by
JOHN MELLENCAMP

THE RAINBOW CONNECTION
from THE MUPPET MOVIE

ALTO SAX

Words and Music by PAUL WILLIAMS
and KENNETH L. ASCHER

RAINDROPS KEEP FALLIN' ON MY HEAD

from BUTCH CASSIDY AND THE SUNDANCE KID

ALTO SAX

Lyric by HAL DAVID
Music by BURT BACHARACH

ROCKIN' ROBIN

ALTO SAX

Words and Music by
J. THOMAS

SAILING

ALTO SAX

Words and Music by
CHRISTOPHER CROSS

SEE YOU LATER, ALLIGATOR

ALTO SAX

Words and Music by
ROBERT GUIDRY

Medium Shuffle

SEVENTY SIX TROMBONES
from Meredith Willson's THE MUSIC MAN

ALTO SAX

By MEREDITH WILLSON

March tempo

SHAKE, RATTLE AND ROLL

ALTO SAX

Words and Music by
CHARLES CALHOUN

SHOUT

ALTO SAX

Words and Music by ROLAND ORZABAL
and IAN STANLEY

SIXTEEN GOING ON SEVENTEEN
from THE SOUND OF MUSIC

ALTO SAX

Lyrics by OSCAR HAMMERSTEIN II
Music by RICHARD RODGERS

Slowly, with expression

SMOOTH

ALTO SAX

Words by ROB THOMAS
Music by ROB THOMAS and ITALL SHUR

SO NICE
(Summer Samba)

ALTO SAX

Original Words and Music by MARCOS VALLE
and PAULO SERGIO VALLE
English Words by NORMAN GIMBEL

Moderately

THE SOUND OF MUSIC
from THE SOUND OF MUSIC

ALTO SAX

Lyrics by OSCAR HAMMERSTEIN II
Music by RICHARD RODGERS

SPINNING WHEEL

ALTO SAX

Words and Music by
DAVID CLAYTON THOMAS

Funky, moderate Rock

SPLISH SPLASH

ALTO SAX

Words and Music by BOBBY DARIN
and MURRAY KAUFMAN

STAND BY ME

ALTO SAX

Words and Music by JERRY LEIBER,
MIKE STOLLER and BEN E. KING

SUNNY

ALTO SAX

Words and Music by
BOBBY HEBB

Moderate Rock

SUPERCALIFRAGILISTICEXPIALIDOCIOUS

from Walt Disney's MARY POPPINS

ALTO SAX

Words and Music by RICHARD M. SHERMAN
and ROBERT B. SHERMAN

SURFIN' U.S.A.

ALTO SAX

Words and Music by
CHUCK BERRY

TAKIN' CARE OF BUSINESS

ALTO SAX

Words and Music by
RANDY BACHMAN

Moderate Rock

TEARS IN HEAVEN

ALTO SAX

Words and Music by ERIC CLAPTON
and WILL JENNINGS

TENNESSEE WALTZ

ALTO SAX

Words and Music by REDD STEWART
and PEE WEE KING

THAT'LL BE THE DAY

ALTO SAX

Words and Music by JERRY ALLISON,
NORMAN PETTY and BUDDY HOLLY

THIS LOVE

ALTO SAX

Words and Music by ADAM LEVINE
and JESSE CARMICHAEL

TIE A YELLOW RIBBON
ROUND THE OLE OAK TREE

ALTO SAX

Words and Music by L. RUSSELL BROWN
and IRWIN LEVINE

TIJUANA TAXI

ALTO SAX

Words by JOHNNY FLAMINGO
Music by ERVAN "BUD" COLEMAN

TRUE COLORS

ALTO SAX

Words and Music by BILLY STEINBERG
and TOM KELLY

THE TWIST

ALTO SAX

Words and Music by
HANK BALLARD

Rock and Roll Shuffle

UP WHERE WE BELONG
from the Paramount Picture AN OFFICER AND A GENTLEMAN

ALTO SAX

Words by WILL JENNINGS
Music by BUFFY SAINTE-MARIE and JACK NITZSCHE

WALKING IN MEMPHIS

ALTO SAX

Words and Music by
MARC COHN

125

THE WAY YOU LOOK TONIGHT
from SWING TIME

ALTO SAX

Words by DOROTHY FIELDS
Music by JEROME KERN

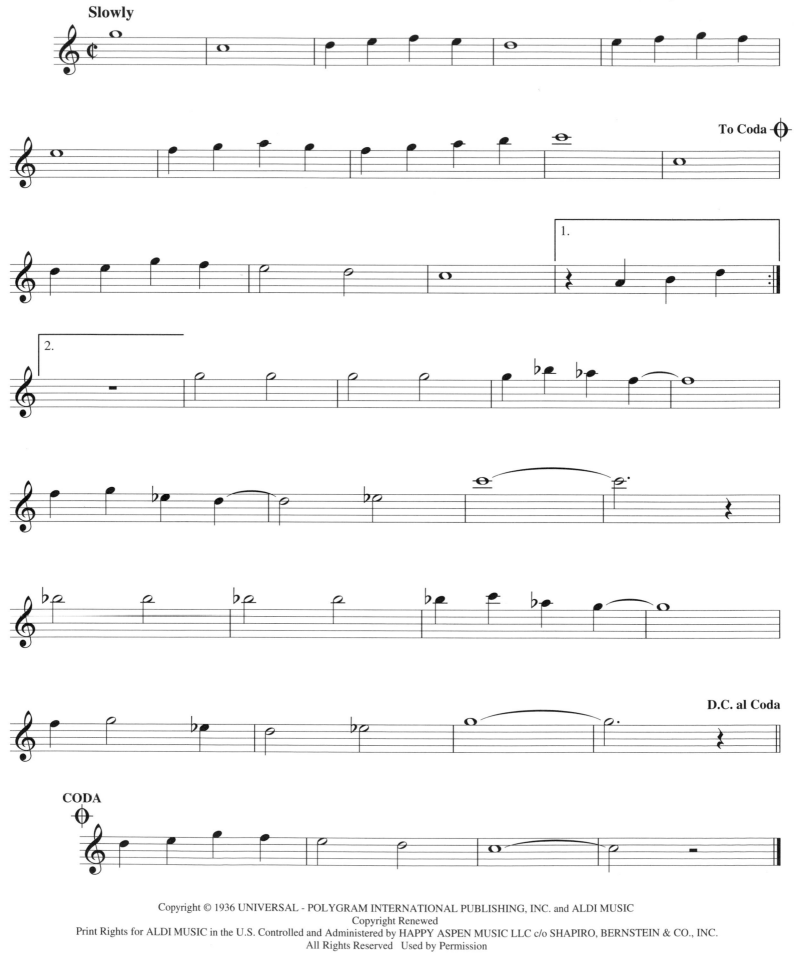

WE ARE FAMILY

ALTO SAX

Words and Music by NILE RODGERS
and BERNARD EDWARDS

WE ARE THE CHAMPIONS

ALTO SAX

Words and Music by
FREDDIE MERCURY

WE BUILT THIS CITY

Alto Sax

Words and Music by BERNIE TAUPIN, MARTIN PAGE,
DENNIS LAMBERT and PETER WOLF

WE'VE ONLY JUST BEGUN

ALTO SAX

Words and Music by ROGER NICHOLS
and PAUL WILLIAMS

WHITE FLAG

ALTO SAX

Words and Music by RICK NOWELS,
ROLLO ARMSTRONG and DIDO ARMSTRONG

A WHOLE NEW WORLD

from Walt Disney's ALADDIN

ALTO SAX

Music by ALAN MENKEN
Lyrics by TIM RICE

Y.M.C.A.

ALTO SAX

Words and Music by JACQUES MORALI,
HENRI BELOLO and VICTOR WILLIS

YESTERDAY

ALTO SAX

Words and Music by JOHN LENNON
and PAUL McCARTNEY

Moderately, with expression

YOU ARE MY SUNSHINE

ALTO SAX

Words and Music by
JIMMIE DAVIS

Lively

YOU LIGHT UP MY LIFE

ALTO SAX

Words and Music by
JOSEPH BROOKS

YOU ARE THE MUSIC IN ME

from the Disney Channel Original Movie HIGH SCHOOL MUSICAL 2

ALTO SAX

Words and Music by
JAMIE HOUSTON

Moderately fast Rock

YOU'RE BEAUTIFUL

Alto Sax

Words and Music by JAMES BLUNT,
SACHA SKARBEK and AMANDA GHOST

YOU'RE STILL THE ONE

ALTO SAX

Words and Music by SHANIA TWAIN
and ROBERT JOHN LANGE

YOU'VE GOT A FRIEND IN ME

from Walt Disney's TOY STORY

ALTO SAX

Music and Lyrics by
RANDY NEWMAN

YOUR SONG

ALTO SAX

Words and Music by ELTON JOHN
and BERNIE TAUPIN

ZOOT SUIT RIOT

ALTO SAX

Words and Music by
STEVE PERRY

Spoken: Blow, dad-dy!

small notes optional